a necklace of knuckles

Letti Lustcraft

For the girl who blamed herself for
what she couldn't change.

And for the ones who read and feel seen.

Contents

red

spiders crawl from
the holes in my head –
sickly fast
synaptic dread;
they stick to my skin
like paper to lead.

"What do you want?"

"We need to be fed."

"What do you eat?"

"Your sticky hot red."

I pricked my thumb
so hard I bled.

"That's not enough,"
the spiders pled.

I pulled out a razor
from under my bed.

1

"That should work,"
the spiders said.

I dragged it deep
the spiders spread
sucking up all my
sticky
hot
red

"Stop," I screamed.
"You'll eat me dead."

euphoric slow and
sickly fed –
the spiders crawled
back in my head.

daddy

This is my fault, too.
These scars that linger and litter my brain,
Refusing to fade - an unfortunate stain.
This is my fault, too.
I've been trying too hard to forget you.

And I do not love you.
I fell in love with your violence -
Your bipolar rage. Your narcissist silence.
Your eyes still stalk my shadows, Viagra blue.
Sometimes I imagine I never did love you.

We danced in dying leaves and déjà vu.
The strobe lights flashed on our haunted house first kiss.
The zombie prisoner writhing in her handcuffed wrists, a
presage wrapped in bloody sheets, out to rescue me and you.
Your poison lips consumed me, and I failed to catch the cue.

I can't believe I ever trusted you.
In October I took orange fist pills in Robbie's backyard,

I hit bottles of whiskey and I fell down hard.
I wanted to do like you do, I wanted to be like you.
I wanted to feel doomed.

I cut my legs with razors and mended them with glue.
You undressed me in the dark, on your California King bed.
You whispered lies and you fucked with my head.
You looked at my scars and I lied to you.
I already told you: This is my fault, too.

If I had the chance I'd choose that night to undo.
You unbalanced my neurons and cut off my tongue.
You fucked me on a barstool and loved me just for fun.
So obviously I fell in love with you,
Just like any dysfunctional teenage girl would do.

But no matter what I did, you wouldn't stay true.
I swallowed my anger and dropped the knife,
I let you win every single fight.
I gave up my friends so I could be with you.
I hurt them so I could be hurt by you.

I dressed up just how you wanted me to.
I called you Daddy and you called me bitch.
I stayed sober while you stayed lit.
I read books to get away from you.
I let you teach me a lesson or two,

You stained my skin red and blue.
I let you build me up so you could beat me down.
I let you choke me and push me to the ground.
I told you that's what I wanted you to do.
Maybe I created the monster in you.

I want you to know this is my fault, too.
We had another dizzy trip around the sun,
I was 17 and you just turned 21.

You lied to me about the party you threw
with benzos and crown and your ex-girlfriend, too.

You told me she was the last thing you'd do.
You said, "She just had a beer and hit the blunt,"
You said, "You should trust me, you little cunt."
A year later I found out you screwed.
I guess on some level I always knew.

I had a lot of firsts while I was with you.
You were the first boyfriend I ever had
who drenched me with jealousy and
loved me like a toy, shiny and new.
Until you got bored once I was used.

The first time I took acid was with you.
Rainbow droplets fell from the sky,
I could taste the salt with only my eyes.
I didn't see Jesus, or Buddha, or Zeus.
Drugs didn't free me or overwhelm me with truth.

I first realized that while I was with you.
You took me on my first highway race,
You dressed me in my first outfit with lace.
You were the first to undress me, too.
But you didn't know that. I lied to you.

A deceitful virgin with a pain virtue.
Alternate endings spin off in my head,
as if we could have been happy instead.
I try to be careful and not let fantasy consume
what will always remain the unbending truth:

Your heart is made of valium and mine of vermouth.
The blend is euphoric but the dangers are vast,
if one heart bleeds more, then the other will crash.
A fizzing chemical mess, spinning us askew.

Just waiting for that dead end drop - ready, set, and doom.

My neurons learned to dance with the abuse.
It became a drug, a dirty dose of degradation.
The exploitation became my foundation.
I built up my walls all around you,
so you could punch through them and savor the ruin.

Despite everything I wasn't, I was never enough for you.
I entertained your desires relating to sex,
I let you degrade me just so you could get
off and I might have an hour or two
when you might not hurt me and you might not loom

over my every stillness and my every move.
The mirror you shattered with the back of my head,
I still see the fractures when I'm alone in my bed.
Sometimes I indulge in the myths of my youth
and I blame that mirror instead of you.

That was the night the stars hid under gloom.
That was the night we ate Xanax and Skyy.
That was the night I forgot how to cry.
I ate one bar, and then you ate two.
I crushed three more and then we blew.

That was the night you knotted the noose.
From that night on, we fell apart
and I stopped believing that you had a heart. But
I crawled on my bloody knees right back, back, back to you.
Only this time you were crawling and bloody, too.

I became indifferent to your insults and I grew
more fond of myself and this power I held
over you. I loved to watch you writhe and
roll in blood and dirt and gobbledygoo.
I loved to poke and prod and torture you,

6

trying to get back, back, back at you.
I must have inhaled your demon, because I know
I wasn't always this way. I wasn't this vengeful
and heartless and full of decay, drowning
so subtly in my own dirty ego and naked truths.

I guess you taught me how to do that, too.
I took drugs to get away from you.
My jaw was locked and my axons were tied
to MDMA in the shape of neon green moons.
I must have been awake for a day or two.

My skin was white and my lips were blue.
After I slept, I said: Never again.
No more drugs. It was time to transcend
you and your friends and all I knew.
I wanted to be nothing like you.

I dressed up just how you never wanted me to.
You called me baby and I called you David.
You grasped at feelings that already faded.
We danced in dying love and déjà vu,
confessing your sins in the closing ballroom.

I took your apologies and marked them with a tomb.

The dance was over but the music kept playing.
I tried to leave but you insisted on staying.
So I pulled your strings and beat your keys,
harmonizing our hopeless melody.

I became numb to the pain
you inflicted on me.
You could hit me severely
but I'd just smile and bleed.
You lost your power over me.

I escaped your grip,
covered in blood and
crescent-nail scars.

You might have stalked me for several weeks,
And I admit that I sort of enjoyed it.
The thrill of driving you so insane
made my broken ego bubble
to a steam.

And I kept thinking words like:

Comic relief.
and
dramatic irony.

And I'm sure you were thinking things like:

Fuck bitches
and
get money.

And I think right now you can probably see
that my life didn't crumble under your demean.

You tried and tried but you never broke me.

So I won't stand by and hold my breath,
waiting for you to say something worth hearing.

And I won't cower away and hold this blame,
thinking you might be someone worth fearing.

Because I think my ghost will haunt your dreams.

And I think right now,

I'm finally free.

spiral

I was once
enchanted,
with your sugared
whispers and
hard candy lies.
Your breath thick with smoke,
I drank in.
Swallowed hard, like
orchestral whisky.
Drunk off your breath,
and your smell –
diesel and
hennessy.
And I must be dreaming,
because you whispered,
softly, your poison lips
just touching my
hot skin.
You said, "Trust me."
So I did.
Your voice resonated
like thunder vibrato,

deep and possessive.
You serenaded
my spine
as the thunder
struck the air.
You led me in circles,
So many circles.
You let me think
that I was
everything,
that we were
anything.
Spiraling into ecstasy,
spiraling into nothing.
Down, down, down…
And you said,
 "Faster now."
Down, down, down…
And I said,
 "Let me out."
Down, down, down…
And I screamed,
 "Is it over now?"
Down…
 Down…
Down…
 It all fades out.

count to ten

One, two...
You tried to run,
but I caught you.

Three, four...
Over my knee,
hands on the floor.

Five, six...
Go ahead, cry,
you'll take your licks.

Seven, eight...
Bare skin red,
keep your legs straight.

Nine, ten...
You clear your mind,
let's go again.

a hot bath

"We forgot bubbles," I frown.
"I'll help you relax,"
A smirk on your lips.
Is this one of your traps?

You draw fever hot water,
Simple and pure.
Until you step in,
then it's not anymore.

You pull me in closer,
I sink into you.
Water rising,
and sin-infused.

Hands on my waist,
they linger then move.
A necklace of knuckles,
I crave the abuse.

Slick areolas

exposed to the air,
squeezed in your grip,
sharp and aware.

An electric ocean,
I'm swimming in you.
Your hot static breath,
power absolute.

over your knee

Over your knee,
I purge my thoughts;
they spill from my eyes,
a storm of salt.

Thundering silence,
the chaos stops –
time is still,
but I am not.

Your hands are lightning,
I squirm and block,
you hold me close,
and I am caught.

My body surrenders,
although it fought;
a surge of power
unravels my knots.

Thread by thread –
my skin burns hot;

endorphin rain pours,
and cools me off.

HTTP 424

My neurons are stuck inside this screen,

eating pixel serotonin

to help feed my self-esteem.

Pandemic solitude

chews and swallows me,

consuming my

sanity.

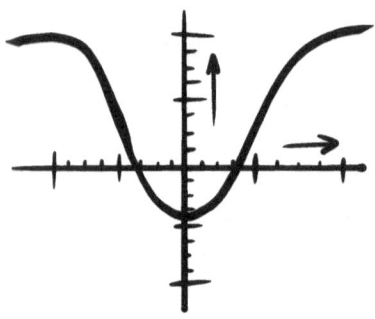

pi

Three point one four one five nine

I count numbers in my head
as you serenade my spine.
You play with me like music -

Two six five three five eight nine

The numbers have a rhythm,
I feel its heartbeat in my core
Chaos beats its hungry pulse -

Seven nine three two three eight four

Your fingers move precisely,
and I burn as you create.
Ravenous circles pull me -

Six two six four three three eight

I calculate my time left
before I melt into you.

Minutes left until consumed.

Three two seven nine five zero two

Bodies like geometry,
making shapes until we're one.
Irrationality drips -

Eight eight four one nine seven one

Our infinity has come

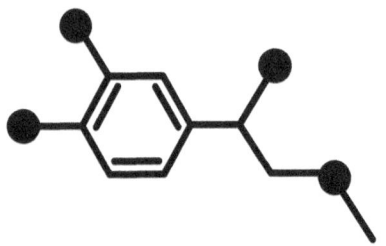

yours

I remembered you with hunger
in my dream last night.
I was yours again –
Special and rare and
held so tight in your fist that
I forgot how to breathe
without your permission.
You kept me hidden,
punished often and pleasured more.
I was yours –
But you were never mine.
I remembered you with passion
in my dream last night.
Poison blue eyes pricking my conscience;
venom flooding my memories with lust.
You held me in your fist
like a demon holds onto dreams even
as I wake, paralyzed and afraid.
Blood rushing. Heart racing.
I used to think adrenaline was love.
Those three seconds
before a climax that never ends

Silent screams. Vision blurred.
I remembered how it felt
to be yours.

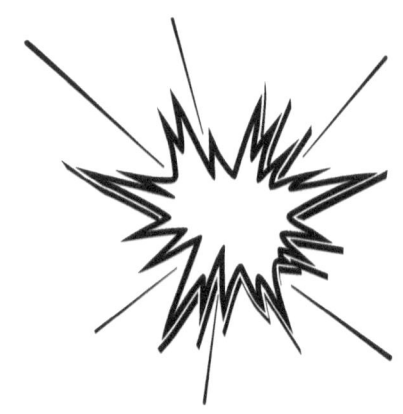

collide

I want to hear
The sound of us colliding.
Your fingers twitch.
You wait for the brat,
or a broken rule.
You'd even take an eyeroll.
I want to feel
my skin blushing,
blood rushing
to the surface;
I want you to feel
my heat entropy.
I want to beg
as you paint a white rose
red with your hands.
I want that whimper
before it lands,
the sound of my submission.
The power I forfeit.
I want that trickle
down my thigh,

the way my body can't hide
the pleasure I feel
when we collide.

roses are violent

cheeks pricked with roses
bloody kisses and wild hearts:
our violent romance

orb weaver

spindled web of knots
tying up her thoughts, sharpens
her gorgeous chaos.

a Sadist's masterpiece

sharp, stinging brush on
sadistcolor skin canvas -
medium of pain.

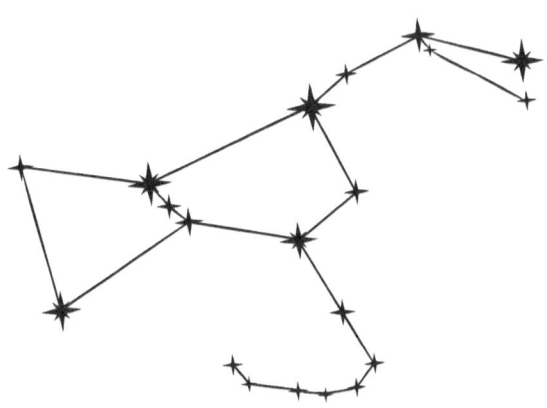

galaxy bruises

capillary stars
ignite her skin, a cosmic
map of sadism.

rigging the moon

suspending the moon -
lunar predicaments in
zero gravity.

Thank you for reading A Necklace of Knuckles.

You can find the author's annotations for each poem,
and the secrets hidden within the syllables, on her website:
www.lettilustcraft.com.

ABOUT THE AUTHOR

Letti Lustcraft is an erotic-romance author and creative whose work focuses on kink positivity and healthy D/s dynamics. She has a masters degree specializing in population health and is passionate about sexual well being and education. Her debut novel, The Brat Diaries, blends erotica with BDSM education to create a reader experience that is both exciting and informative. In the vast sea of smut, Lustcraft makes a conscious effort to contribute realistic dynamics, consent, and risk-awareness to the genre.

Find out more about her upcoming projects at
www.lettilustcraft.com